IT'S TRUE! We Came From slime

Other  titles

Ken McNamara

PICTURES BY Andrew Plant

IT'S TRUE!

We Came From slime

annick press

toronto + new york + vancouver

For Jean Radford

for her endless support and encouragement

Copyright © text Ken McNamara 2006
Copyright © illustrations Andrew Plant 2006
Series design copyright © Ruth Grüner 2006

Annick Press Ltd.
First published in Australia by Allen & Unwin.

We acknowledge the support of the Canada Council for the Arts,
the Ontario Arts Council, and the Government of Canada through
the Book Publishing Industry Development Program (BPIDP)
for our publishing activities.

Proofread by Elizabeth McLean
Production of this edition by Antonia Banyard
Cover photograph: Photodisc Collection/Getty Images
Set in 12.5pt Minion by Ruth Grüner

Cataloging in Publication
McNamara, Ken
It's true! we came from slime / by Ken McNamara ;
illustrated by Andrew Plant. — North American ed.

Includes bibliographical references and index.
ISBN-13: 978-1-55037-953-2 (bound).—ISBN-13: 978-1-55037-952-5 (pbk.)
ISBN-10: 1-55037-953-4 (bound).—ISBN-10: 1-55037-952-6 (pbk.)

1. Evolution (Biology)—Juvenile literature. I. Plant, Andrew II. Title.

QH367.1.M35 2006   j576.8   C2005-906267-3

Printed in Canada

1 3 5 7 9 10 8 6 4 2

Published in the U.S.A. by
Annick Press (U.S.) Ltd.

Distributed in Canada by:
Firefly Books Ltd.
66 Leek Crescent
Richmond Hill, ON
L4B 1H1

Distributed in the U.S.A. by:
Firefly Books (U.S.) Inc.
P.O. Box 1338
Ellicott Station
Buffalo, NY 14205

Visit our website at: www.annickpress.com

Contents

Why life before dinosaurs?

I've been collecting fossils since I was nine years old. Most people grow out of this when they become adults. I never did. I still get a kick out of discovering a new one and knowing what amazing creature made it, eons ago.

In this book you'll discover some strange animals that lived in the sea half a billion years ago (one looked like a vacuum cleaner with teeth and five eyes). You'll find out about scorpion-like animals bigger than you, insects as big as parrots and spiders as big as cats (it's true!). You'll find out who, or what, your long-lost ancestors looked like, and whether we really did come from slime.

Join me on a 3-billion-year journey through time and discover how all these strange creatures evolved on Planet Earth.

Chapter 1

Concrete cauliflowers

Life on Earth is always changing. A hundred million years ago, dinosaurs tramped through the forests. But long before that, an amazing number of animals wandered and slithered over the land, or swam and crawled in the seas. And if we went right back in time, we'd find that the very first creatures, thousands of millions of years ago, were so small that you couldn't see them. All you'd see is just a bit of slime . . .

Do you like cauliflowers? I do, so I'm going to begin with them. What on earth, you might ask, do cauliflowers have to do with life before the dinosaurs?

It's a fair question. But, strange as it might seem, even a cauliflower has a part to play in this story.

If your fridge is anything like mine, there'll be all sorts of strange and not so wondrous things lurking inside. Perhaps there's a cauliflower that's been sitting in there, minding its own business, for weeks. Rather than the crisp, snowy white ball that went in, it is now a crusty black lump that looks as though it's about to crawl out of the fridge on its own. This rather smelly object looks uncannily like some rocks that grow in shallow bays and lakes in places like British Columbia, the Bahamas and Western Australia. These rocks are called stromatolites (stro-**mat**-o-lites), and they are very peculiar, not just because they look like concrete

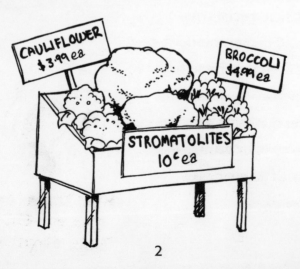

cauliflowers, but because they grow. That's right, a rock that grows. And, believe it or not, these rotten cauliflower look-alikes are the key to understanding the very first life on Earth.

Bugs that rock

Like the cauliflower, when it was once happily living in a field of cauli cousins, stromatolites get energy from the Sun. This is because these rocks are made by bugs —actually, a special type of bug, called *cyanobacteria* (that means blue-green bacteria). Yes, bacteria—those invisible creatures that make a nuisance of themselves by getting up your nose and giving you a cold, or worse.

Uh oh! No way am I going up THERE! That's disgusting!

Some are a bit more choosy about where they live and hang out in the sea or in lakes and have this clever way of making rocks. (And aren't you glad this type don't live up your nose?)

Snug as a bug in mud

These bugs are slimy, so any mud floating in the water sticks to them. They are also able to cement mud grains together (which is why you wouldn't want these bugs living up your nose). Adding mud grain to mud grain, they build up stromatolites about as high as your knee. That's pretty impressive for a bug so small that when you sneeze it out of your nose it's traveling at about 160 kilometers (100 miles) per hour. It's like humans building a small mountain (and we haven't managed that yet). In the lakes and shallow bays where they are found, these rocks are slowly growing—cementing mud day by day, century by century. Many are more than 1000 years old. And these little bugs, or ones just like them, have been doing this for a very, very, very long time—3500 million years, in fact.

O.K, O.K,
we don't need granite benchtops.
But does EVERYTHING have to be made of mud?

Now, you might think it's been a "long time" since you last put on a clean pair of socks, but we're talking a *seriously* long time here—a mind-bogglingly huge amount of time that's almost too big to think about. We can talk about dinosaurs first appearing about 230 million years ago and humans just a few hundred thousand years ago, but what does it really *mean*?

OK — 3500 million years — a bit boring, guys, let's try evolving a little .... guys?.. Some evolution here, O.K?.... guys .... hello?

Here's a way of thinking about it that might help. Hold this book in one hand. Keep reading. Stretch your other hand out to the side. Yes, right out, pointing your fingers. Now, just imagine that your nose represents when life began on Earth. (I said *when* it began—not *where*.) In this book we are going to travel from your nose, across your face, down your arm, as far as the beginning of your fingers. That would represent when dinosaurs first appeared, around 230 million years ago. They became extinct at the beginning of the last joint of your finger. Humans appeared just a few hundred thousand years ago—they are the thinnest piece of fingernail you can snip off.

In this first chapter we are going to travel a long way —from the tip of your nose to your wrist. And, as we shall see, for much of this extremely long period of time (from about 3500 to a little under 600 million years ago), there wasn't much on this Earth, except for bugs, bugs and more bugs—oh, and lots of slime.

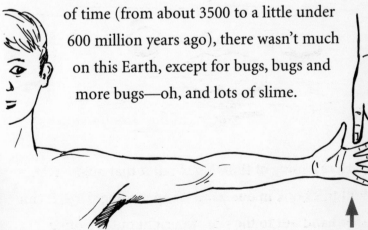

Dinosaurs appear

Bugs and breakfast

If you look at a map of Australia, the big lump in the
top left corner is the Pilbara region. Here all is red,
green and blue—the red of the rocks, the green of
the prickly spinifex grass and the blue of the sky.
In some of these red rocks we find the oldest fossils
in the world. But they are not fossils of bones or
shells. Amazingly, they're fossilized stromatolites,
a bit like the ones still growing today in other parts
of Western Australia.

In the 1980s, scientists collected some dark gray,
flinty rocks that are found with the fossil stromatolites.
They cut the rocks with a special diamond saw, into
really thin slices, thinner than tissue paper—slices so
thin you can see through them. Then, using a very
powerful microscope, the scientists were able to find
the actual fossilized remains of the bugs that made
the stromatolites.

We owe a lot to these bugs, particularly the
cyanobacteria. Incredible as it may seem, they gave us
the oxygen we breathe. Even more surprisingly,

they made the mountains of iron ore in the Pilbara. These are mined and turned into the cans that contain the baked beans you had for dinner and the car you were driven to school in.

Speaking of baked beans . . . Before there was oxygen in the air, a few thousand million years ago, there was a lot of methane. (That's the unmentionable gas that appears when you've eaten too many baked beans.) There was also a lot of another gas, carbon dioxide. Like plants today, the ancient blue-green bugs turned the carbon dioxide into sugars, using energy from sunlight. A side product was the gas oxygen.

When these bugs first started doing this, oxygen bubbled into the sea. This caused iron minerals dissolved in the sea to turn into rust.

Oops! Pardon me!

For hundreds of millons of years the sea continued to produce rust. These iron-rich muds have since turned into the great mountains of iron ore that today are mined in the Pilbara, to make your baked bean can, your parents' car, and so on.

The little bugs kept on soaking up the carbon dioxide and spitting out the oxygen. Once the air became rich in breathable oxygen (probably about your shoulder on our trip down your arm), some of these simple bacterial cells came together, some living inside others. And so evolved slime and the first seaweeds (near your elbow). Some time after that, though we don't know exactly when, other cells got together and made cells that later evolved into the first animals.

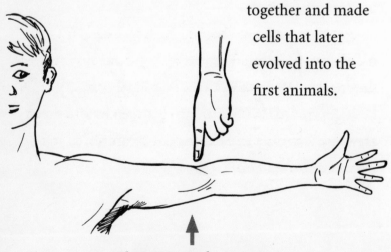

First seaweeds appear

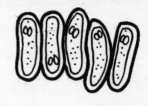

Hanging out with your friends,
"making seaweed," were you?

("Evolved" means "changed over a very long period of time"—see pages 12–13.) We are still hunting for their fossilized remains. Maybe they are so tiny that we won't be able to find them.

So we owe a lot to those early slimy bugs. Not only did they give us the air we breathe and our tin cans, but they're also **our extremely long-, long-, long-lost ancestors**. In between us and them are some fearsome and far-fetched creatures, as you'll see when you read on.

MAKING EVOLUTION HAPPEN

By looking at fossils of different ages we can see that animals, plants, fungi and bacteria have changed —very, very slowly—over time. We say they have "evolved," and we call this slow process of change "evolution." So how does evolution happen?

Well, imagine two tigers racing to catch an antelope. The one that is the better hunter—maybe the one that runs faster—will get to it first and then have some food for its cubs. It is more likely to survive and raise young. At least some of the cubs will be like the parent—they'll be successful hunters. Gradually more and more of the surviving tigers will be faster runners. Over time they may become so different from the original tigers that they no longer breed with them, and so a new species evolves.

Similarly, fish with teeth and jaws evolved from the earliest fish that had neither. Teeth made these later fish more successful at catching their prey.

This has happened for other animals, and plants as well. The ones best equipped to get food or avoid being eaten are the ones best suited to their surroundings, and so they survive and multiply. The English scientist Charles Darwin was the person who worked out how evolution happened. He called it "natural selection."

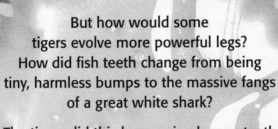

But how would some
tigers evolve more powerful legs?
How did fish teeth change from being
tiny, harmless bumps to the massive fangs
of a great white shark?

The tigers did this by growing legs or teeth
a little faster or a little longer, and ended up
bigger and more powerful. The fish did it much
the same way with their teeth. These changes
were then passed on from parents to offspring
over many generations.

In the 1930s scientist realized that what we look
like and how fast we grow was determined by
chemical messengers in our cells, called genes.

So three things make up evolution:
natural selection; changes in how fast
and for how long we grow; and genes
that pass these changes on
to the next generation.

Chapter 2

Awash with gutless wonders

You are very annoyed. You spent yesterday planting 25 daffodil bulbs for your mom. Today is her birthday. Okay, the chance of there being 25 bright yellow flowers nodding and smiling in the breeze was pretty low. But it's the thought that counts. Just give them a couple of months. You went out into the garden to check your handiwork. And that's when you saw the mess. Your beautifully prepared garden has been dug up by the neighbor's dumb cat! He's dug a hole so deep that it looks as if he's been digging for gold.

Half of your carefully planted bulbs have been dug up and kicked far and wide. Even worse, after doing his evil, smelly business in the hole he didn't even cover it up properly. Yuk.

So what's this got to do with fossils? Quite a lot, actually. Firstly, the word "fossil" comes from the Latin word *fossilis*, meaning "dug up"—just what the cat did. A lot of words in paleontology (the study of ancient life) come from Latin, which is not surprising, really. It's a dead language, and fossils are very, very dead! But the other thing about your exploded flowerbed is that you have assumed the cat did it. Did you see the cat do it? No. Then how do you know it was the cat, and not some half-crazed leprechaun looking for gold? You know because, like a detective and like a paleontologist, you've used clues to work out who did the evil deed. What you have is some disturbed soil—and the cat's poo. That's evidence enough.

Tracking trails and traces

Amazing as it may seem,
the oldest known
animal fossil has
something in
common with the
cat's nighttime
adventure. This very old
fossil is called a trace fossil,
because it records the traces

Trace fossils of
party behavior

of animal activity. Not all fossils are parts of a creature,
such as bones or shells. Some, such as dinosaur
footprints, or the trails left in the sand by some little
worm, are trace fossils. If your daffodil bed somehow
amazingly got preserved for millions of years and
turned into rock, then the cat's diggings would be a
trace fossil. They may not tell us much about what the
animals looked like, but trace fossils tell us a lot about
how they behaved. No, I don't mean whether they were
good or bad, but whether they crawled or slithered or
burrowed—things like that.

For thousands of millions of years there were no other life forms on Earth but bugs. Lots and lots of bugs. From the tip of your nose until about your elbow, there were just bugs. Then came the seaweeds that I mentioned before. We've found fossil remains of them. Sometimes we see them as spirals in 2000-million-year-old rocks, other times as little rows of beads in rocks 1500 million years old in Glacier National Park, Montana. This is long before any animals showed up.

Then we see the first trails and scrapings made in sand by animals, and somehow amazingly preserved in rock for about 700 million years. They are like a faraway snapshot in time. Unlike your cat, we have no idea what the animal looked like that left its trail in the sands of an ancient sea. It was probably something like a tiny worm. More recent trace fossils left by animals often form complex patterns, like spirals, or form burrows in the sand. This shows us that the animals that made them were changing and becoming more complex over millions of years. This is evolution at work again.

Fossil air mattresses

To find out what the first animals actually looked like, we have to travel a little further in time, down to your wrist—that's about 550 million years ago. We've found some of these very strange-looking fossils from this period in Canada and around the world in places like Russia and Namibia. They are called "Ediacaran" fossils and are named after the settlement nearest to where they were first found in the Flinders Ranges in southern Australia. They are the remains of very strange creatures, rather like air mattresses and tires, though a bit smaller. Some resemble jellyfish and are as big as a dinner plate. Others are similar to long strands of puffy seaweed

First animals appear

and were as long as a cat. Some may have been worms; others look like nothing still living today.

The man who first discovered them was a geologist called Reg Sprigg. When Reg was exploring in the Flinders Ranges in the 1940s, people thought the rocks were so old there wouldn't be any fossils in them. Nobody seems to have told Reg, because he found hundreds, and more than a dozen different types.

A little while after, in the early 1960s, a schoolboy called Roger Mason discovered a fossil in England that looked just like one that Reg had found. A keen collector, Roger also went looking for fossils where there weren't meant to be any, in a place called Charnwood Forest. What he found was an amazing fossil—like a big leaf. This was another of these strange, animal-like Ediacaran fossils.

As with all animals and plants, whether living or fossil, it was scientifically described and given a name, *Charnia masoni*. All living things have two names. The first is the genus name; the second the species name. Your dog is *Canis familiaris* (and where was it when that pesky cat was in your garden?). A wolf is very similar to a dog and is in the same genus, but it has a different species name, and so it is called *Canis lupus*. It's a bit like your name, but the other way round. Your "genus" name is your family name, the same as your mom's and dad's. Your "species" name is your own—Tim, Katie, Carlos, Farouk, whatever. So when Roger Mason's fossil was formally named, it was given its own genus name (*Charnia* after Charnwood Forest), while the species was named after its finder, and became *masoni*.

Canis familiaris

Canis **un**familiaris

Ediacaran fossils have since been found in many other parts of the world, and all in rocks of the same age. And all of them are gutless wonders. I'm not meaning to be rude here, it's just that even though the fossils are well preserved, paleontologists can't find any sign of a mouth, or a gut, or an anus.

So how did these creatures feed? How did they digest their food? How did they go to the toilet? The answer to all three questions is the same: we don't know. Perhaps they just soaked up food through their skins.

Trust me – we don't need a toilet.

One scientist has suggested that maybe the Ediacaran fossils weren't animals at all, but lichen. These are the green patches you sometimes see on rocks—they grow so slowly they make sloths look like Olympic sprinters.

Another scientist has suggested that the Ediacaran fossils were neither animals nor lichen. He thinks they may have been a form of life quite different from anything living today.

Whatever they were, they seem to have lived a peaceful, quiet life, gently floating around in warm, shallow seas. But this idyllic life was soon to be shattered. Some creatures appeared that changed the whole course of life on this planet for the next 500 million years. These were animals that were fed up with eating sushi (seaweed). They had taken a fancy to sashimi (raw seafood). **The first meat-eaters had arrived.**

Chapter 3

Eat or be eaten

The worm never saw it coming. Silent but deadly, the *Anomalocaris* appeared from the dark blue, deep water. As large as a fox, it looked like a cross between a crayfish and the starship *Enterprise*. Hanging from its body were more than 10 pairs of paddles, which it used to glide with ease through the water. It fixed its large eyes on a wormy breakfast, then spread out two huge claws, ready to pounce.

The worm didn't stand a chance. Strong claws gripped it tight and pulled it from the burrow in which it was hiding. If the worm had had eyes, the last thing it would have seen would have been a vicious mouth getting larger and larger—a mouth that looked exactly

Predator?
Yeah, right! They haven't
even evolved yet!

like a pineapple ring with teeth. **Predators had arrived on Earth.**

After 3 billion years (your nose to your wrist) of just slimy, gooey bugs and seaweed, and the weird Ediacarans, the seas were now teeming with all kinds of marine animals, from clams and snails to crayfish-like creatures and worms of many shapes and sizes. Some animals had begun to eat each other. Eating mud and sucking on slimy seaweed had somehow lost its appeal.

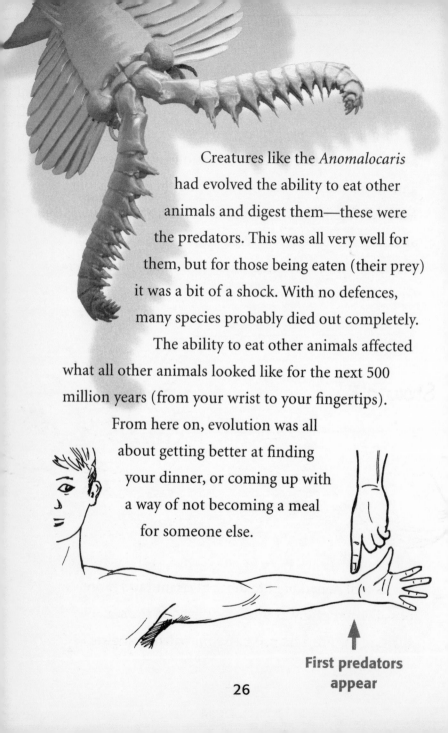

Creatures like the *Anomalocaris* had evolved the ability to eat other animals and digest them—these were the predators. This was all very well for them, but for those being eaten (their prey) it was a bit of a shock. With no defences, many species probably died out completely.

The ability to eat other animals affected what all other animals looked like for the next 500 million years (from your wrist to your fingertips). From here on, evolution was all about getting better at finding your dinner, or coming up with a way of not becoming a meal for someone else.

First predators appear

26

Fossil armor

The only way for prey to survive was to come up with a way of protecting themselves. And many did this in a most spectacular way—by growing their own armor. Many different kinds of animals came up with this amazing ability—they learned how to grow crystals that could transform into hard shells and protect them from the new predators.

Show-off!

As well as making life more pleasant (and more possible) for many animals that lived in the sea, shells made life a lot more fun for paleontologists.

Searching for fossils in older rocks is hard work—we might find a few stromatolites or, if we're incredibly lucky, an Ediacaran fossil. But in rocks less than 545 million years old, it's so much easier. In these "young" rocks we can find fossils of animals with shells.

It makes sense that hard parts of animals are more usually preserved than soft parts. Drop a donut into the sea and it will turn into mush fast. It is most unlikely to end up as a fossil. However, if you drop in something hard, it's a different story. If you could grab back one of your first teeth from a tooth fairy and chuck that in the ocean, it would have a much better chance of being fossilized. So, for animals that crawl and burrow through soft muds or sands, there's a far greater chance of their hard shells becoming fossils when they die than their soft parts. Shells can last for years before becoming buried in mud or sand and then preserved in a rock as a fossil.

Trilobite "cookies"

There is another reason why one type of animal that lived at this time is often found fossilized. And that's because of how it grew. These animals were trilobites. They were once very common, but they all died out (became extinct) about 250 million years ago. (This is about where your fingers join on to your hand, just before the first dinosaurs appeared on Earth.) Trilobites belong in the same group as insects, spiders, crabs and prawns—the arthropods. All these types of animals have "segmented" bodies.

So, what is a segmented body? Well, for a trilobite, just imagine a plastic package of cookies. If you take all the cookies out of their wrapper, but leave them resting in their plastic tray, then each cookie is a bit like a segment of a trilobite. Joined to each trilobite segment was a pair of legs. So a trilobite with 10 body segments had 10 pairs of legs.

Fortunately, cookies rarely have pairs of legs, so they remain in their tray. Trilobites, though, probably scuttled over the sand on lots of little legs. Now imagine that your cookies are chocolate-coated. Six at one end got warm and melted a bit. As they cooled, they stuck together. The rest of the biscuits are loose. Trilobites were like that (although not, so far as we know, chocolate-coated). They have a head formed from six segments joined together as a head shield.

Like all living arthropods, trilobites peeled off their old shells every so often as they grew. A new, slightly larger shell had been growing underneath. Imagine chucking off all your clothes and finding another, new set. That's what it was like for the trilobite. This means that if a single trilobite shed its skin, say, 20 times during its life, it could leave 20 fossilized heads, hundreds of body segments and 20 fossilized tails—all left in the mud for a paleontologist to find hundreds of millions of

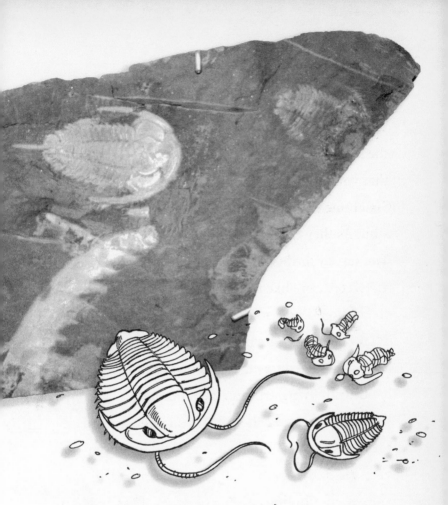

Just LOOK at your room!

years later. It's like throwing your clothes on your
bedroom floor and leaving them for your mom to pick
up—but she never does, and they stay there forever . . .

If you have to hunt for your food, or you want to avoid being eaten, it's useful to be able to see. Trilobites had the *best* eyes. Their two eyes were made of hundreds of tiny lenses, each made from a single clear crystal. One American paleontologist found out that he could attach one of these little crystalline lenses to a special camera and take a photo through it. So, 350 million years after a trilobite was using it to look for its last meal, the paleontologist was using it to take a photo out of the window of his laboratory. It came out really well, showing that trilobites had great vision. Best of all, I think, is that the photo was of the FBI building across the road. The home of America's special police force was being spied on by a trilobite!

Digging for fossil worms

Let's go back to Tuesday, August 31, 1909. A man was looking for fossil trilobites high in the Rocky Mountains in British Columbia. His name was Charles Doolite Walcott, and with the help of his wife and son he had been finding trilobites in this area for some years. As Mrs. Walcott was riding along a narrow track on a steep mountainside, her horse suddenly stumbled on a large rock. Walcott jumped off his horse and smacked the rock hard with his hammer. Inside were the fossilized remains of some strange wormlike creatures. What Walcott had stumbled on (or more accurately, what his wife's horse had stumbled on) turned out to be one of the most important and richest fossil deposits ever found. Over the next few years Walcott and his family collected tens of thousands of fossils from these rocks, called the Burgess Shale. Almost 100 years later, paleontologists are still studying the fossils that the Walcotts found.

In these rocks were the remains of not only trilobites' hard shells, but also their legs. Sometimes their last meal was preserved in their stomachs. Walcott found many different types of beautifully preserved worms, including ones that were covered by lots of spines; in some you can even see their blood vessels. There were lots of different arthropods, including the huge *Anomalocaris* that I described at the start of the chapter. Some were very strange indeed. My favorite is a beast no longer than your middle finger and called *Opabinia*. Segmented like your plastic package of cookies, this strange animal had five big eyes on stalks. Where its mouth should be there was a long nozzle, like a vacuum cleaner, with teeth on the end.

What are you staring at?

If I had any eyes, I could tell you!

Another strange animal, about the size of a quarter, we've called *Wiwaxia*. It was covered with large armor plates, and had a whole load of blades like steak knives sticking out of its back. Eating this beast would have been a painful, big mistake. We are not sure what type of animal it was. Maybe a strange worm; maybe a strange sort of clam. But the animal that really takes the cake when it comes to weirdness is like your worst nightmare—all spines and long legs with a blob for a head. And this explains its name—*Hallucigenia*. ("To hallucinate" means to imagine strange, distorted things.) Fortunately, it was only about as long as your thumbnail.

Upside down? I don't even know which end I'm talking out of!

Chapter 4

"My, what strange teeth you have, Grandma"

Bones are very useful. Without them you'd be in a sorry state. Leap out of bed first thing in the morning and, thanks to gravity, you'd end up on the floor as a rather sad pile of floppy skin and quivering muscle. Luckily, you *do* have bones. You, along with all other humans, belong in the group of animals known as "vertebrates" or "backboned animals." This includes mammals, reptiles (snakes and lizards), amphibians (such as frogs) and fish.

Evolving a backbone

The first vertebrates were very strange. This was because they *didn't* have a backbone at all. What makes them a vertebrate is a thread, called a notochord, that ran down where their backbone would have been. Fortunately for them, they lived in the sea, so they didn't need a backbone so much. The sea held them up. So, why do scientists think that they had backbones? Good question.

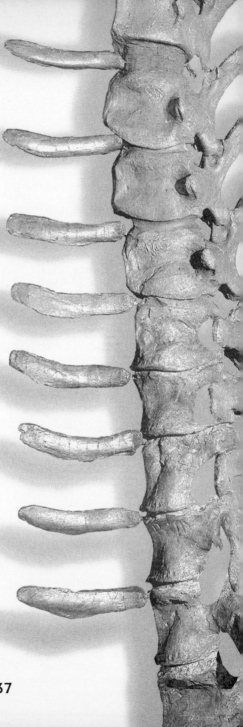

The oldest vertebrate fossils were fish. Now, when you think of a fish you probably imagine something covered in batter, snuggling up to a pile of french fries, and sprinkled with salt and lemon juice. Surprising as it may seem, this isn't a bad picture of what the first fish looked like more than 500 million years ago. Okay, you can take away the fries (or better still, eat them), and imagine that the batter was its skin. (We'll come back to the lemon juice later.) What's inside the batter is fish flesh. The next time you tuck into your plate of fish and fries, look carefully at the fish. It's not a solid, single lump of flesh. You'll see that you can pull it apart into segments. If your piece of fish is large enough, you'll see that each of these segments is V-shaped.

Good heavens! This fish died after being a-salt-ed and battered!

This is one of the things, along with the notochord, that makes the fish a vertebrate. And your piece of fish from the grocery store is unlikely to have a backbone, just like the first fish fossils.

These oldest of all fish fossils have only just been discovered, near a place called Chengjiang in southern China. These first fish swam in the sea with *Hallucigenia* and *Anomalocaris*. They are called *Myllokunmingia* and *Haikouichthys*. As well as not having a backbone,

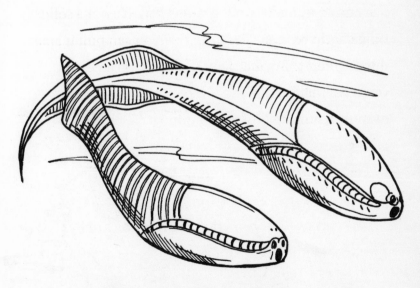

Oh yeah? So bite me!

these fish didn't have any teeth or jaws. They couldn't even have given you a gummy suck, let alone a bite. They did have fins, though.

Sixty million years later (that's about 480 million years ago), fish had begun to look a bit more fishlike. At this time, a shallow sea covered much of North America. While trilobites crawled over the mud and sand at the bottom of this sea, fish called *Astraspis* and *Eryptychius* swam above them. They had a few fins, so they could swim reasonably well. These, and other fish of the time, were certainly strange. Even though they still didn't have jaws, they did have teeth. Mmmmm. So where do you think they kept them? Weird as it may seem, they wore them on their bodies, which were covered by hundreds of tiny toothlike scales. As you can imagine, these scales or teeth were no use for biting or chewing. It is more likely they formed an armor that helped protect the fish from being eaten. Trying to chew and swallow something covered by hundreds of teeth could be a bit painful.

Then one of evolution's miracles occurred.

Fish began to grow bony jaws, and these coats of teeth moved from covering the fish's body to living in their bigger mouths. Now the teeth could be used for biting. With strong jaws and pointed teeth, these new fish became predators, feeding on smaller, toothless fish, and probably on prawnlike crustaceans.

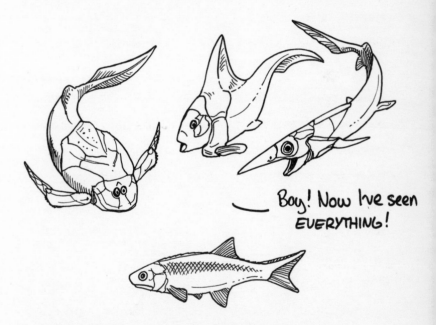

Boy! Now I've seen EVERYTHING!

One thing these early fish still didn't have was a real backbone. They did have one of sorts. But the trouble was that instead of being made of hard bone,

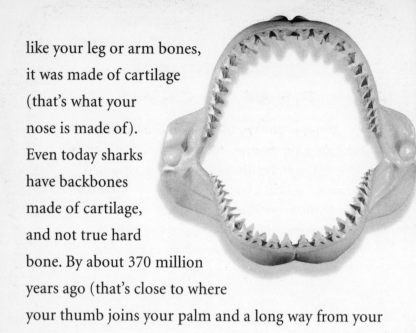

like your leg or arm bones,
it was made of cartilage
(that's what your
nose is made of).
Even today sharks
have backbones
made of cartilage,
and not true hard
bone. By about 370 million
years ago (that's close to where
your thumb joins your palm and a long way from your
nose where life began), so many different types of fish
had evolved that they ruled the seas. They left so
many fossils that this time is sometimes
called The Age of Fish.

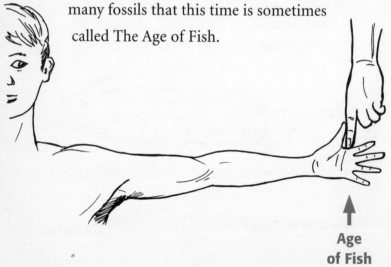

**Age
of Fish**

SOMETHING'S FISHY IN CHINA

A name like *Myllokunmingia* probably sounds a bit strange. It's a mixture of Chinese and Greek words. The scientists who first named this fish used the name of a nearby town, and the Greek word *myllos*, meaning fish. Kunming is the capital of Yunnan Province in China.

The species name of the fish is *fengjiaoa*, which comes from the Chinese word *fengjiao*, meaning "beautiful." So *Myllokunmingia fengjiaoa* really means "beautiful Kunming fish."

Haikouichthys is another Chinese and Greek word. It means "Haikou fish." Haikou is the town near where the fossil was found.

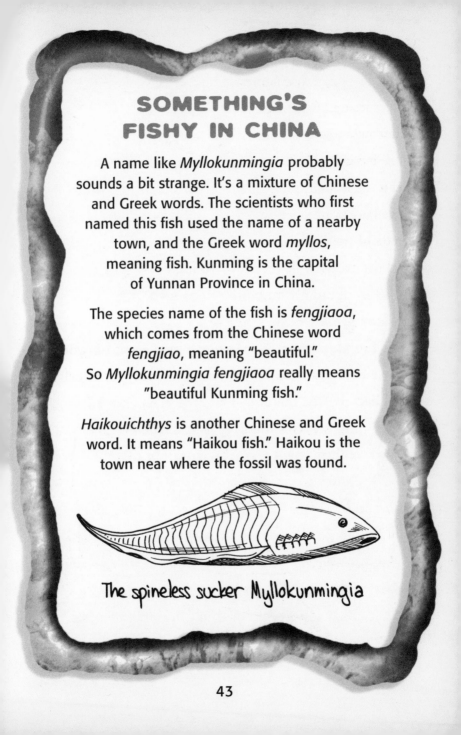

The spineless sucker Myllokunmingia

Gogo fish

The best examples of fossil fish anywhere in the world are in Australia, in the Kimberley region of Western Australia. These are called the Gogo fish. You probably imagine that collecting fossils is all about hitting a rock as hard as you can with a hammer and hoping that it breaks in half to reveal a fossil. Well, that's how fossils are usually found. But it's a lot harder to get the best out of the Gogo fish. The fossilized bone is locked inside a hard lump of limestone rock. If you hammer hard enough to break open the limestone, you might break the fossil.

There's another way of getting to the fish fossils. The bone, amazingly, hasn't changed in over 370 million years and is still original bone, so you can put weak acid on it and it won't dissolve. The limestone rock, though, will slowly dissolve away in acid. It's a bit like putting an ice cube in warm water. Over a few minutes it would melt. You can do this for yourself. Put a bit of broken chicken bone in an ice-cube tray—freeze it, then drop it in warm water.

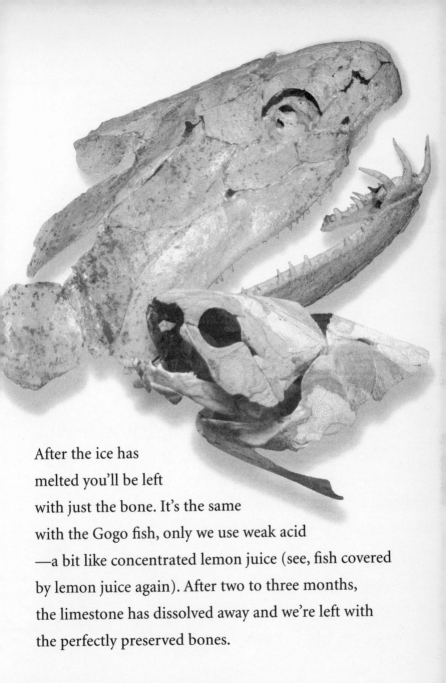

After the ice has
melted you'll be left
with just the bone. It's the same
with the Gogo fish, only we use weak acid
—a bit like concentrated lemon juice (see, fish covered
by lemon juice again). After two to three months,
the limestone has dissolved away and we're left with
the perfectly preserved bones.

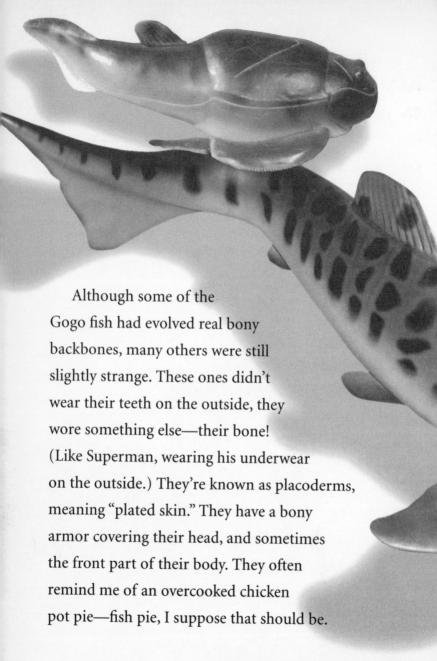

Although some of the
Gogo fish had evolved real bony
backbones, many others were still
slightly strange. These ones didn't
wear their teeth on the outside, they
wore something else—their bone!
(Like Superman, wearing his underwear
on the outside.) They're known as placoderms,
meaning "plated skin." They have a bony
armor covering their head, and sometimes
the front part of their body. They often
remind me of an overcooked chicken
pot pie—fish pie, I suppose that should be.

At this time (near your thumb, remember), sharks were tiny, not much bigger than snapper. The placoderms ruled the seas. Some grew as long as a stretch limo. We know that these fish ate other fish because of a fossil discovery. After dissolving one of these limestone rocks a paleontologist found a placoderm head, but it wasn't alone. Stuck in its mouth was the head of a smaller fish. Almost certainly the larger fish's eyes were too large for its belly and it choked to death on the smaller one.

"JUST CALL ME KEN"

You might wonder why we call fossil fish "Gogo fish." It's because they were found near a big ranch called Gogo Station. One of these Gogo fish has become very well known in the part of the world where it was found. In 1994, a group of students from an elementary school in Australia thought that the state they lived in should have its own fossil emblem, just like American states do. After looking at photos and drawings of Gogo fish, they chose one and wrote to the state officials. On December 5, 1995, the governor officially made it the state fossil emblem of Western Australia.

Just call me Ken!

The fish the students chose is called *Mcnamaraspis*, which by an amazing coincidence is my surname. Okay, it's not really a coincidence. The fish had been named after me in 1995 by my colleague John Long, who discovered it. This was my 40th birthday present from him. It was certainly my most unusual birthday present, that's for sure. Little did I realize then that "my" fish would become Australia's first state fossil emblem.

Chapter 5

Stepping out

Bullies: you know what they're like—always trying to push you around, and always bigger than you. You can try and ignore them, but they never seem to go away. Some of the smaller animals swimming and crawling in the ancient seas had a worse problem. One false move and they could end up as the bullies' breakfast.

One way to avoid hungry predators like this was to escape to somewhere they couldn't follow. And this is just what some animals did nearly 500 million years ago, by taking their first steps on land. From the time when life first evolved, animals had lived in the sea. But then some arthropods (those animals with lots of armored legs and crunchy outer shells) were able to spend more time out of water. So they could more readily escape from the large animals that were forever trying to eat them.

Rows of holes in sand

Fossils of the first land animals have been found in Western Australia and in Canada. These are not fossils of the animals themselves, though. They are the tracks left behind as the animals scuttled along wet, sandy beaches under the blazing sun.

Working out what type of animal
made the tracks is usually not easy.
If you are about to get into your car
in the morning and see muddy footprints on the hood,
you can usually tell straightaway that it was that pesky
cat again. Each animal leaves its own special footprint.
The cat footprint is quite different from that of a duck,
for instance (though why a duck should be waddling
over the front of your car beats me). But the footprints
of the first land-dwellers aren't so easily identified.
These creatures all had legs that looked much like
crab's legs, so all they left was rows of holes in the sand.
And when you've seen one
hole, you've seen them all.

It's some kind of horrible monster!

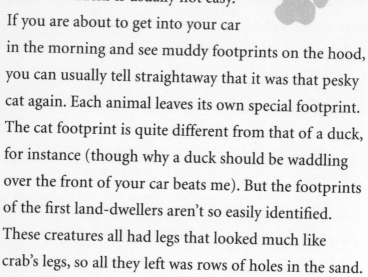

The only difference between various ancient arthropod footprints is in how many groups of holes they made. This tells us how many legs they had, and so we can tell them apart. Think of arthropods today. An insect has three pairs of legs; a millipede can have over a hundred.

Sunbathers, watch out!

The trouble with bullies is that they often find ways to track you down. So, not long after the little arthropods escaped from the sea, the big bullies soon found a way to follow their breakfast onto dry land.

Fossilized tracks show that some pretty impressive beasts were tramping along sandy river banks about 450 million years ago. Some tracks were made by centipede-like animals, as long as a big dog. The most frightening were the eurypterids—animals that you definitely would not have wanted to encounter when they were looking for lunch.

If you were ever able to hop on a passing time machine and travel back all these hundreds of millions of years, the one thing you really wouldn't want to do is suntan for too long. This is in case you're joined by a eurypterid, otherwise known as a "giant sea scorpion." That last word is enough to scare the pants off some people. Put "giant" in front and we are in a whole new state of terror. These beasts grew to 2 meters ($6^1/_2$ feet) long. That's right, a scorpion-like animal about as long as Michael Jordan.

We're fairly sure that these huge creatures were ferocious killers. Some were armed with a pair of fearsome, crablike pincers that they could use to grab their prey. Others had huge, needlelike claws that locked together to form a cage in which their next meal

could be trapped. They probably killed it by stinging it with the tip of their tail, in the same way that scorpions do today.

The only good thing is that for these big brutes, moving around out of water was probably not very easy. They were used to being supported by the sea all around them. You probably know what it's like. You can lie in the sea and float, but if you try lying in air you will quickly come down   to earth with a bump. It's called gravity. They probably moved very slowly on land, and so they would have found it hard to run as fast as their breakfast.

Footprints to fossils

One of the mysteries of paleontology is how footprints made by an animal hundreds of millions of years ago could ever survive long enough to be preserved as a fossil. When you walk along a beach, you leave some perfect footprints in the sand (so long as the sand is not too wet or too dry). But once a wave comes in, they're washed away.

The eurypterids that have left their tracks in sandstone were probably staggering slowly across wet sand. At this time, more than 400 million years ago, few plants grew on land. There were no trees, no grass, not even any cauliflowers. This means that there was hardly any soil. Whenever the wind blew there would have been dust storms, the same as today when the wind blows across dry, newly plowed fields. This very fine sand would have gently settled on the eurypterids' footprints, covering them up. When the sand eventually turned into rock, the footprints were preserved. Wind, rain and flowing rivers exposed the footprints for paleontologists to find. Whenever I find one

I am always amazed I am looking at footprints showing the movement of an animal for perhaps one minute of its life, preserved like a snapshot for hundreds of millions of years.

Fish fingers do the walking

It took another 100 million years before the descendants of fish took their first steps on land. These were the amphibians. But I suppose the fish can be excused. You can't develop legs overnight.

First came some fish that had evolved arm bones, exactly like yours and mine. But fish fingers didn't exist hundreds of millions of years ago, either in the frying pan or on a fish. Instead of fingers, they still had fins. Not much use for picking their noses, that's for sure. Then some other animal called *Acanthostega*, living in what is now Greenland, grew fingers from its hands instead of fins. Unlike your five digits (four fingers and a thumb), they had eight fingers on each limb. I wonder whether the decimal system that we use for counting (10 years in a decade and so on) developed because on our two hands we have 10 digits.

Maybe if these early amphibians had developed the ability to count it might have been based on 16 rather than 10. It seems unlikely that these animals could have spent much, if any, time on land. The fossils show they still had gills like fish, so they must have continued to live in the water most of the time.

Eventually species evolved that had limbs strong enough to support their weight on land. The problem then was breathing. Fish breathe in water using gills. Humans breathe in air using lungs, like all other animals with backbones. Fossils don't show us how this evolution from gills to lungs took place. But it's obvious that it did happen.

These strange fish with limbs were able to spend more and more time out of water. Eventually some began to live in one of the newly growing forests that were beginning to clothe the land. **The first land vertebrates had finally arrived.** And from these, millions of years later, evolved dinosaurs and birds, hedgehogs and humans.

So, a fossil fish looking at you from a display case in the museum may be one of your ancestors—your great-great-great . . . (roughly 100 million greats) grandparent. If you see one, don't forget to say, "Hello."

Chapter 6

Up, up and away

One of the best things at a fair, I think, is the bumper cars. You push your foot on the accelerator, the car lurches forward, and *bump*! You smack into someone else. Strange as it may seem, there is a link between bumper cars, mountain ranges, coal, electricity and . . . insects the size of large parrots!

When you run into someone in your bumper car, you just bounce off. But if you didn't, what would happen? You've locked bumpers and you're pushing harder and harder into each other. You can't both go down, as the floor is in the way. All that leaves is for one or both of you to tilt up. The front of the bumper cars would rise, very slowly at first, then faster, until you ended up pointing to the sky.

Crusty continents

Imagine that you're riding on something a bit larger —say a continent like North America. (You really don't have to imagine it, because this is actually what you are doing as you read this book—being taken for a ride on a continent. Every morning when you get out of bed, you and your bed have moved a tiny bit during the night.) For the last 150 million years, the North American land mass has been moving steadily westwards at about the speed that your toenails grow— about 2 centimeters ($^3/_4$ inch) a year. Perhaps one way to work out how far we've traveled is to never cut your toenails (except that it wouldn't be too popular with your parents). If your nails had never been cut, you could measure how far you'd gone since you were born. In 150 million years North America has traveled 3000 kilometers (almost 1900 miles) from Africa and

Europe, to which we were once joined. Since I was born, North America has traveled just over 1 meter (²/₃ mile). How far has it gone since you were born?

North America isn't the only continent that's doing this. They all are—sliding around the globe, like bumper cars in very slow motion, or like a herd of elephants randomly sliding on their bums across a frozen lake. Every so often they bump into each other. They can do this because the hard rock that makes the continents is semi-floating on a layer of molten rock that is almost liquid (something like porridge). The hard rock on top is called the continental crust. I know this makes it sound like some kind of bread, but that's really what it's called.

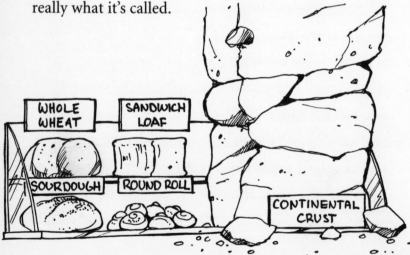

WHOLE WHEAT

SANDWICH LOAF

SOURDOUGH

ROUND ROLL

CONTINENTAL CRUST

India, for example, is pushing into Asia. And the more it tries to shove its way north, the higher the Himalayas get. As with the bumper cars, the only way to go is up.

Imagine you have a carpet on a shiny wooden floor. If you run hard until you land on the carpet, you'll go sliding along the floor. When the carpet hits the wall it will rumple up into folds, like a very small mountain range. (Better not try this one, because you and the wall could collide quite hard!)

Greenhouse world

When continents bump into each other, splits appear in the Earth's crust. Molten rock (lava) either shoots or oozes out of the splits, forming volcanoes. Huge amounts of gas are released with the lava and ash. Much of this is carbon dioxide. The more of this gas that gets into the air, the warmer the Earth gets. This is known as the Greenhouse Effect. (A greenhouse is a little shed made entirely of glass. This keeps the plants inside it warm and they grow faster, so the shed ends up looking green. For some reason it's not called a glass-shed, but a greenhouse.)

Some fossil plants show us that around 340 million years ago (quite close to your knuckles), there was far more carbon dioxide in the air than there is now. Earth must have been much warmer then. It was also a lot wetter—hot, steamy and tropical, in fact. The plants grew fast and furious, and the Earth became clothed in green. Great forests grew. Plants that today are little bigger than carrots grew to more than 30 meters (100 feet) tall. In the undergrowth moved the first reptiles, descendants of the amphibians that had left the rivers and lakes. Reptiles no longer had to stay in water to breed, as amphibians did. They had evolved eggs with hard outer skins that didn't dry out.

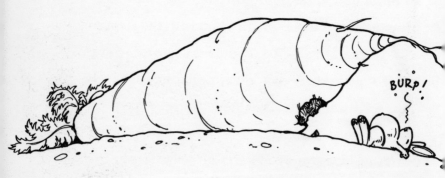

BURP!

FOSSIL LEAVES TELL A STORY

Plants "breathe" through their leaves using tiny holes called stomata. During the day they take in carbon dioxide and give out oxygen. (When we breathe, we do it the other way round.) The more carbon dioxide in the air, the fewer stomata that the plants need. By comparing fossil leaves with modern leaves, we can work out how much carbon dioxide was in the air millions of years ago.

The biggest animals to make their way through the dense ferns were animals called arthropleurids (**ar**-thro-plur-ids). They looked like centipedes, but were as long and fat as a pig. The real novelty, though, was a sound that Earth had never heard before—the sound of wings beating rapidly in the thick, hot air. **Animals had conquered the skies.** The first to do this were insects.

The earliest insects were very similar to silverfish. Silverfish are those shiny little insects that you sometimes see scurrying out from under a book or some old paper. They can't fly, so they are easy to catch.

But you try catching a fly or a dragonfly. It zips past you so fast you can hardly see it. The insects that took to the air were better able to escape their predators.

Some of the earliest insects got very, very big. This would have also helped stop them being eaten. Among the oldest flying insects are some dragonflies that had wingspans of over 70 centimeters (28 inches) —that's about the same as a cockatoo. A spiderlike animal living at this time was up to 35 centimeters (14 inches) long. Its name is *Megarachne*, which (surprise, surprise) means "giant spider."

Arachne means spider, just add Mega! Think about it. A spider the size of a small cat. Perhaps better not to think about it?

The forests that these animals lived in were so dense and grew for so long that over millions of years they built up layer after layer of rotting leaves, branches and trunks. Eventually these hardened and turned into coal. The same thing happened again about 60 million years later, when huge forests covered the continents. Half of the United States' and one-fifth of Canada's electricity comes from coal. So the electricity that powers the light you are reading this book by (assuming of course that it's nighttime) may come from burning the remains of plants that lived hundreds of millions of years ago.

So, there we have it. There is a link between bumper cars, mountain ranges, coal, electricity and insects the size of large parrots. You didn't believe me, did you?

Chapter 7

First prize in the ugly competition

Imagine a creature built like a small tank and with the temperament of a cranky grizzly bear. The enormous mouth bristles with teeth like steak knives. It's hard to imagine how it could have closed its mouth without stabbing itself in the nose and jaw at the same time. Waddling along on huge feet and looking as though it was wearing an oversized baseball mitt on each hand, this creature from hell was top dog on land 250 million years ago. It is called a gorgonopsid.

Gorgonopsids were just one of a whole zoo of very weird reptiles that had spread far and wide across the world. You might think that dinosaurs were a pretty strange-looking bunch. They had nothing on these animals, though, which ruled the world for about 100 million years, long before dinosaurs appeared on the scene. What's more, you and every mammal that's ever lived evolved from these animals.

Sail of the century

These mammal-like reptiles spread right across a single great land mass called Pangaea, between 320 and 220 million years ago. (We've finally arrived at your fingers.) One of the first mammal-like reptiles was one of the most peculiar. Known as *Dimetrodon*, it was about the size of a dog, but with shorter, stubby legs, like a crocodile. The really odd thing was the huge, finlike sail on its back. Extremely long, thin spines stuck up from the animal's backbones. Between them was a thin membrane, like the sails of a yacht. (If they ever got caught on an iced-over lake on a windy day, they would probably have broken the land speed record.) The sail wasn't there to speed up the movement of *Dimetrodon*, though.

Mammal-like reptiles appear

Fossils show that the bases of the spines were packed with a rich supply of blood vessels. The sail probably worked like a reverse-cycle air conditioner.

If *Dimetrodon* stood sideways to the sun in the early mornings, it would quickly warm up. If it got too hot, it could turn away from the sun, or find some shade, and it would lose heat through these huge sails. Like lizards and snakes today, these animals were cold-blooded. That's why we still call them reptiles, even though they were in some ways similar to mammals.

Dimetrodon was one of a group of animals called pelycosaurs. While some pelycosaurs were peaceful plant-eaters, others, such as *Dimetrodon*, were fierce meat-eaters. *Sphenocodon*, for instance, was as large as a lion, and had a mouth crammed full of sharp, vicious teeth. Other pelycosaurs, called ophiacodonts, seemed to think they were crocodiles, living for much of their time in the water. They had a long snout, studded with many sharp, peglike teeth. Their eyes were set high on their head, so they could peek out of the water while being almost totally submerged.

Therapsids (the what?)

By about 265 million years ago (round about your knuckles) most pelycosaurs had died out. Replacing them were a new group of mammal-like reptiles, called the therapsids (not a word to say first thing in the morning with a mouth full of granola). These little beauties would have given the gorgonopsids some competition in any ugly contest. Some had a bulky body, stubby legs, short tail and oversized head, often with protruding fangs that probably dripped buckets of drool. Many looked like a cross between a hippopotamus and a crocodile.

The therapsids were much more mammal-like than the pelycosaurs. The world in which they lived was warmer, so they didn't need a built-in radiator to warm them up in the mornings. The first therapsids were small, lightly built animals, and almost certainly efficient killers. Many had long snouts packed with a fearsome array of teeth that allowed them to neatly slice flesh from their prey. Unlike their lumbering pelycosaur relatives, who had slowly waddled along, these therapsids had limbs set beneath their bodies, rather than outwards. Because they stood more upright, they could run fast.

Not all therapsids were meat-eaters. It wasn't long before plant-eaters evolved. Some, like *Estemmenosuchus* from Russia, were oxlike, with horns protruding from their heads. One, called *Moschops*, was the size of a small elephant. Instead of a trunk it had a large, parrot-like beak. Later ones that lived about 220 million years ago had much smaller heads.

Just think!
We're the peak of mammal evolution!

The most common were the dicynodonts (which means they had a pair of tusk-like teeth). Their other teeth were really tiny and useless. Some may have lived in the water, like hippos. Others may have burrowed in the ground, like gophers.

The most mammal-like of the later meat-eating therapsids were the cynodonts. These were doglike animals that had long legs and short tails, and bodies that may well have been covered in fur. If you could

have peered into their mouth, without having your
nose bitten off in the process (or fainting at the smell,
like four-week-old meatloaf), you would have seen that
their teeth were quite like yours. They had molars for
chewing, and canines (your Dracula teeth) and incisors
(the ones you use, but shouldn't, for biting your nails).
The tooth fairy of the time would have been extremely
overworked, because cynodonts shed teeth and
replaced them with new ones throughout their lives.
This is something reptiles do. We change our teeth only
once, like other mammals.

Mammals finally arrive

Many changes occurred to the mammal-like reptiles before they eventually evolved into true mammals. But what made the first true mammals different? Mammals have larger brains than snakes and lizards, and give birth to live young (except for echidnas and platypuses, which lay eggs). What really makes cats, rats, you and me different from therapsids, lizards and snakes (apart from not usually being especially slithery and scaly) is that we are far more active and create our own high body temperature. We don't need to wear a solar panel on our back. We just need to eat a lot more food, in fact, about 10 times as much as a reptile of the same size.

By having legs slung under their bodies, later therapsids could travel farther and faster. The trouble with being on the go all the time was that the animals needed to eat a lot more to keep their energy levels up. So they had to spend a lot more time looking for food. To be so active they also needed to breathe in more oxygen. Therapsids evolved the knack of being able to eat and breathe at the same time, an ability they passed on to mammals. The evolution of the different types of chewing, gnawing and biting teeth meant that food could be broken up and chewed more effectively before being swallowed. This reduced the chances of getting indigestion. So when your parents tell you not to bolt your food, but to chew it properly before you swallow, they're following some good advice first developed more than 200 million years ago. (No, this does not mean that you can accuse your parents of being that old.)

Changes in the way that later therapsids and mammals fed meant changes to the shape of the jaw.

Ugh! You eat like a mammal!

As well as chomping up and down, you and I can also move our jaws sideways while chewing. Reptiles can't do this. The jaw of a reptile is made up of lots of different bones. Mammals evolved single, large upper and lower jaw bones, strongly hinged together.

Some of the smaller bones didn't disappear completely, though. They ended up in your ear, of all places, where they got a new job, forming the three bones of your inner ear. This gave mammals much better hearing, a useful thing to have if you are a meat-eater listening for its prey, or its prey listening out for a pair of flying fangs trying to bite you in the bum.

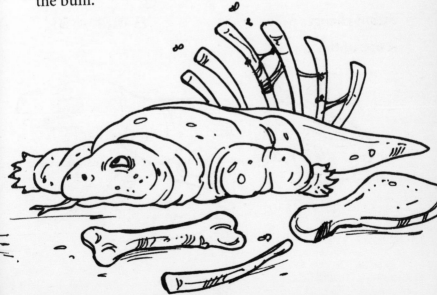

Therapsids eventually lost out to dinosaurs in the battle for survival. But they had the last laugh.

They passed on all these useful features to some tiny, shrewlike mammals that were forever getting under the dinosaurs' feet. And when the dinosaurs died out, 65 million years ago, mammals took over. So therapsids set the stage for the stunning explosion of mammals that took place during the last 60 million years.

You'll see! We're going to take over, I tell you. We're going to rule the world!

In this new world dominated by mammals, including humans, the flying insects were joined by birds, and flowering plants grew everywhere—grasses, cherry trees, carnations and, of course, cauliflowers.

That's O.K. I can wait!

So there we are. We began with bugs. Bugs evolved into seaweeds and slime, which evolved into animals, which evolved—into you! **It's true: we came from slime.**

Timeline

MILLION YEARS AGO	▶	EVENT
3500	▶	Earliest evidence for fossils— stromatolites made by microbes
2000	▶	First seaweeds
550	▶	Ediacaran fossils —the gutless wonders
530	▶	First trilobites and other fossils with armor
520	▶	Soft-bodied fossils from the Burgess Shale
450	▶	Arthropods—first animals to walk on land
370	▶	Gogo fish and first vertebrates on land (amphibians)
340	▶	World's first forests and first flying insects
320	▶	First mammal-like reptiles
230	▶	First mammals and first dinosaurs

Where to find out more

Books

Judy Cutchins. *Giant Predators of the Ancient Seas*. Sarasota, FL: Pineapple Press, 2001.

Richard Fortey. *Fossils: the Key to the Past*. Washington: Smithsonian Institution Press, 2002.

Steve Jenkins. *Life on Earth: The Story of Evolution*. Boston: Houghton Mifflin, 2002.

Cyril Walker and David Ward, *Fossils*. London: Dorling Kindersley, 2002.

Websites

General sites on fossils:

- www.paleoportal.org
- http://evolution.berkeley.edu
- www.fossilmuseum.net

On trilobites:

- www.enchantedlearning.com/subjects/invertebrates/trilobite/Trilobiteprintout.shtml
- www.trilobites.info

On Burgess Shale fossils:

- www.geo.ucalgary.ca/~macrae/Burgess_Shale/

Museums

There are lots of museums that have good displays of fossils, including the Royal Tyrrell Museum (Drumheller, AB), The Museum of Paleontology, (University of California, Berkeley, CA), The Dinosaur Museum (Blanding, UT), The Dakota Dinosaur Museum, (Dickinson, ND), the American Museum of Natural History (New York, NY), and the Smithsonian National Museum of Natural History, (Washington, DC).

For teachers

Derek Briggs, Douglas Erwin and Frederick Collier. *The Fossils of the Burgess Shale*. Washington: Smithsonian Books, Washington, 1995.

Richard Dawkins. *The Ancestor's Tale: A Pilgrimage to the Dawn of Evolution*. Boston: Houghton Mifflin, 2004.

John Long and Ken McNamara. *The Evolution Revolution*. Chichester: Wiley and Sons, 1998.

Frank Rhodes, Paul Shaffer and Herbert Zim. *Fossils*. New York: St. Martin's Press, 2001.

Index

About the author and illustrator

KEN McNAMARA has been collecting fossils for so long he almost feels like one at times. He is very happy to work as a paleontologist at the Western Australia Museum in Perth, where they pay him to spend time on his hobby. As well as collecting fossils, studying them, writing scientific papers and books about them, he and his colleagues have put a great display of them on at the museum called "Diamonds to Dinosaurs."

ANDREW PLANT has been drawing fossils, and the creatures that left them behind, almost since he first picked up a crayon. In fact, he'll draw just about anything, and has also written a few books to put the pictures in, as well as illustrating a bunch of other people's books. He also teaches schoolkids about dinosaurs at the Monash University Science Centre in Melbourne, Australia.

Thanks

I am very grateful to my wife, Sue Radford, and my children, Jamie, Katie and Tim McNamara, for reading the book and gently telling me when I was getting too fanciful with my writing. Thanks to Marcus Good for help with websites. Thanks to Sarah Brenan for her careful and perceptive editing of the manuscript, and for finding such a talented artist as Andrew Plant, who clearly sees ancient life in the same way that I do. I am also grateful to Cheryl Silcox and the students of Helena Valley Primary School for their very helpful feedback on the book.

Ken McNamara

Andrew Plant would like to thank Ken McNamara for having the same weird sense of humor as he does. "If he wants to name a cyanobacterium after me, that'd be really cool."

Andrew Plant

The publishers would like to thank istockphoto.com and the photographers named for images appearing on the following pages: pages viii, 12–13, 48–49 Dan Brandenburg (background); pages 13 and 42 Rob Stegmann; page 14 Diane Diederich; page 15 James Hernandez; page 35 istockphoto.com; pages 37 and 52 Pascal Le Brun; page 42 Rob Stegmann; page 56 Jocelyn Banyard (Michael Jordan); page 67 Mike Brittain (modern leaf). Thanks also to BrandX Pictures, Bugs and Insects collection, for those on pages 19 (magnifying glass), 53, 68; Dr John Long for the one on page 82; and Ken McNamara for the remainder.